C

Cooking, Canning, Chickens, Compost, Camping, Checklists and Car Kits

By

Lisa Goodwin

Copyright Information

Legal Disclaimers

About This Book

About eight years ago, I remember searching the internet for information related to prepping after getting curious of this way of life. The curiosity grew, as did my own desire of becoming more self-sufficient. The internet offers a wealth of information, either be blogs, or Q and A's of others who are looking for the same information. Do a Google search of "How to Prep" and you will get over sixty-six million results. If you get more specific with your searches, you will get even more results. By the time this book is published, it will be even more.

This is the third book in this series, and it seems with each letter, I am finding more and learning more information to share with others in what it means to prep, or be more self-reliant. I do realize it is impossible to live and be totally self-sufficient. That is a completely unrealistic expectation, and if that is yours, you may be a little disappointed in this series.

However, if you are looking for some information that you may not find on the internet, then this may be a great book series for you. Just like you, I am always learning, and putting those things that I learn into practice. We van always learn more, and become better at the skills we already know by gaining information, and then putting that information to practice.

I am not going to use a lot of frightening statistics, or graphic pictures to scare you into reading this. There is enough fear created in this world, and I do not mean to add to it. I don't believe shock and awe tactics work in order to get others interested in becoming prepared and more self-sufficient.

There are enough books available that do that. My goal is to make you think, and plan accordingly. Statistics will not help you to survive, but basic knowledge can put the odds in your favor. With knowledge, skills and preparation you can and will survive, and may even thrive. This means not only being prepared physically, with supplies, and such, but even more importantly you will need to be prepared mentally.

This entire series will be broken down into letters of the alphabet, and what you can do to prepare and plan within each letter of the alphabet. In the end, if you read all 26 books, I promise you will have a very good comprehension of what it means to be prepared, and will also have a lot of information that will help you to become more self-reliant

Preparing and planning can seem a bit overpowering when you first start out. Just keep in mind you will be always planning and preparing from this point on so going at your own pace is smart, and advised.

In order to be prepared for an emergency situation, your mind has to be constantly thinking, "what if?" You need to be thinking one-step ahead, and planning of how you will react to any given situation. Like the other books, I have included what if scenarios for you to think about, but I have changed it up a little bit, starting with this book. One of the most important parts of being prepared is knowing what to do in a stressful situation. And although most situations will not be an end of the world as we know it situation, even just knowing how to deal with what life throws at you on a daily basis will help to keep you more prepared for even bigger situations.

Let's take a "what if" scenario to get your mind thinking.

What if you move to a rural area to get away from the life of the big city, or even suburbia. You are excited to start working the land, and have visions of a bountiful harvest from your fist attempt at a garden. You have big dreams of not only supplying enough food for your family and close friends, but think maybe you will have so much you can even sell some of your harvest.

You read all of the books about gardening, and are so excited when you see some little plants starting to break through the ground, not many, but a few. You keep watering and working the plants without much luck. Getting frustrated, you turn to using fertilizers and commercial feeds in order to help your garden. But no matter how hard you work at it, your harvest is small, and not even enough to break out your new canning equipment. What went wrong?

Or, another situation, you decide you want to add chickens to your preparedness lifestyle. But where do you begin? You have never had taken care of anything other than your family dog. But where do you buy chickens? How much care do they need? Are you even allowed to have them in your neighborhood? What does it mean to care for chickens, and how do you handle the eggs they will produce?

And going off a little deeper on that subject...

You have been learning to live a more self-reliant lifestyle. You have a pretty good food pantry built up, and you have even started your own flock of chickens. But know the economy has collapsed, food prices are skyrocketing on a daily basis. You are feeling a little better about things because of your chickens and food storage. But you can't help but think about all of those who don't have a lot, and your neighbors are going hungry. Do you feel you can help out a few friends or neighbors? How could you manage giving a little to others?

And just one more scenario for you to think about. You have committed to your family and yourself, that you are going to be more prepared, and you are going to keep more food. But things are really tight. There seem to be so many bills to pay, and you have three credit cards that are almost maxed out. You barely have enough money to get through the month, let alone start a stockpile of food and supplies. How are you going to make that happen?

These are very realistic scenarios that could happen to you, your neighbors, or your loved ones. These may not seem like end of the world situations, but to you, they could severely impact your motivation to become more prepared. Prepping is becoming more popular with many people as they feel something is just not right with the way our country, and our world is running today.

With a little planning and some practice, you can be prepared for any of the above situations and many, many more. That is what this book is meant to do, help give you situations and practical tips you can apply to almost any situation in order to be more prepared.

By being prepared for any situation, you will not only help yourself and your loved ones, but you might be an asset to your neighbors, and even your community. By reading this book, you are giving yourself an advantage at emergency and even everyday life preparedness. You will have the tools and the information to help make you more self-reliant and self-responsible.

COOKING, CANNING, CHICKENS, COMPOST, CAMPING, CHECKLISTS AND CAR KITS

Cooking

Cooking and canning go hand in hand when it comes to being prepared, but chickens? Compost, and checklists? Yes, chickens composting and checklists! When looking at all aspects of being prepared, each of these topics could actually have huge volumes completely dedicated to each individual subject.

Cooking is a part of all of our daily lives. Some may be good at it, while others need more practice. With a lot of practice, you can hone your cooking skills into cooking as a prepper.

When cooking, there are items you need for any recipe you are creating for it to turn out correctly. There isn't really any difference in prepping and cooking. Before you cook, you prep. The difference comes in the planning. But in a grid down, or SHTF scenario, how will you cook for yourself and your family? No matter what is happening, we all need to eat. In a stressful situation, it is even more important to keep your body nourished in order for you to be functioning at your best capacity.

Cooking in difficult times can create a sense of familiarity, peace, and comfort. But depending on the situation, how you go about cooking might change a little bit. Thinking outside of the box is helpful when it comes to cooking. There are different ways to cook outside of using the standard oven and microwave so many of us take for granted will always be there, and look at it as the only option. So let's say your electricity is out, or your stove and microwave are no longer working, what would you do? Here are some options:

1. Solar Ovens

A solar oven is just what its name implies. An oven uses the energy of the sun to bake or cook food. There are many different versions that you can purchase, however, it is possible to build your own as well.

Materials needed:

A reflective accordion-folding car sunshade

A Cake rack (or wire frame or grill rack)

6 inches of self-adhesive backed Velcro

Dutch oven (cast iron)

Plastic tote or basket (even a plastic trash can)

A large clear plastic baking bag

Lay the sunshade out with the notched side toward you.

Cut the Velcro into three pieces, each about 2 inches long.

Evenly space your Velcro, onto the edge to the left of the notch (at the middle of the sun shade); and attach the matching half of each piece onto the underneath size to the right of the notch, so that they fit together when the two sides are brought together to form a funnel. You don't have to use the self-adhesive Velcro, you could use craft glue if you only have plain Velcro, just make sure it is attached really good.

Press the Velcro pieces together, and set the funnel on top of a bucket or a round or rectangular plastic wastebasket.

Place your Dutch oven on top of a square cake rack, placed inside a plastic baking bag. A standard size rack is about ten inches. This is placed inside the funnel, so that the rack rests on the top edges of the bucket or wastebasket. Since the sunshade material is soft and flexible, the rack is necessary to support the pot. It also allows the rays of the sun to shine down under the pot and reflect on all sides. The funnel can be tilted in the direction of the sun.

If it is windy, you can place a stick across from one side of the funnel to the other to help keep it stable and open. With the weight of the cast iron Dutch oven you should not have to worry about it blowing over, even if it is windy.

When you're done cooking, all you have to do is fold up your 'oven' and slip it into the trash can along with your rack and store it away until you need to use it again.

This little oven is practical and easy to use. It will not cook as fast as your conventional oven would, but if you don't have a stove for whatever reason, this will work in a pinch!

So far with a little practice, and a lot of sun, I have gotten my solar oven up to 375 degrees. This may be due to our elevation, and the amount of sun we get, but it does work. I have cooked beans, scalloped potatoes, brownies, vegetables and even boil water.

The sunshade may not be available everywhere, but you can always find them on the internet. The Velcro is available at dollar or fabric stores and of course, online. Cost of the sunshade was about $5.00(I found mine on eBay for $4.35 and free shipping) and the Velcro about $.75, the cooking bag is a plastic bag, which I got for about $.50. So for less than ten dollars, you have created your own oven that uses no electricity.

2. Camp stove

Camp stoves are great, you can use them in place of a regular stove, as long as you have the fuel source. These little stoves can always be found at yard sales for around ten dollars. I have run across them at thrift stores as well. If you are not able to find one in your area, you can purchase them new for around seventy dollars, but too me that seems like a waste of my money, and my limited budget for prepping. It's better to save money by spending a little extra time searching for the great deal. The bottles of fuel run about two dollars and last a long time, well worth investing in.

3. Backyard grill

Don't overlook your trusty grill! Most people have grills, whether they are propane or charcoal, a grill is a grill! Use your grill just as you would your stovetop for cooking food, boiling water, and of course grilling your meat. (Remember to keep it outside of course.)

And almost any food can be cooked over the grill wrapped in aluminum foil, fruits, vegetables, and meats. It will also keep your grill cleaner, and no grease for you to clean up off the grill!

4. Fireplace/Wood burning Stove Insert

Don't forget your fireplace, if it's wood burning. Start a fire, and cook right in the fire. Wrap up your food in aluminum foil, and place it in the fire. You can also place on top of the grate in the fireplace. Another option is if you have a wood burning stove insert. These are great! The not only create heat, but the top can serve as a cook top as well. If you have a fireplace that you are able to put a wood burning stove insert into, you can find them on Craigslist for cheap, sometimes even free, if you have the muscle to help you get it home.

Cast iron pots, frying pans, tortilla pans, and Dutch ovens

are great items to search for at the thrift stores and yard sales. Yes, of course you can buy them online, but why? You can find them all over the place for cheap.

5. Solar Water Lens

Although not as practical as some of the other cooking applications, this could be one worth looking into depending on what area of the world you live in, and at what time of day you are going to be cooking. But basically, you create a disk with water in plastic (clear) that has been rigged up so the water forms a "bowl" or lens. Think about it like this, when you were a kid, did you ever pick up a magnifying glass and burn ants? That is the same principle that the "Aqua Lens" uses to cook food. The sun's rays are intensified through the "lens", and whatever is below it, gets cooked.

It is possible to cook your meals like this, however, the sun needs to be overhead for a longer period of time, so if you are closer to the equator, you will have more success than if you were in the far northern United States. And although it may not be a great option, it is an option, and worth looking into. This isn't for everyone, but it is an option that you could cook with, if you have the time to create the giant lens.

There are a lot of videos on YouTube, and more information on the internet if this is something you would like to try.

6. Volcano Grill (Stove)

This stove is the coolest thing I have ever seen! The Volcano stove is a product that uses three different types of fuel sources. It can be used with propane, charcoal or wood. This stove is lightweight and versatile making it a great alternative way to cook. With the multiple options for fuel sources, this little stove can be used in many different ways. The stove is collapsible, making it easier to pack up and move, or just keep it stored until you are ready to use it. You can cook directly on it, like a grill, or you can use pans, like a stovetop, or you can cook in a Dutch oven, utilizing it like an oven.

These stoves are a great option, and are a little expensive in my opinion, but it would be a good investment that would pay for itself in times of need. At the time of writing this I found it online for $169.99, and that includes a propane attachment on eBay. Emergency Essentials website has it for $195.00 including shipping. It is helpful to know that the places I found to purchase this stove offer the propane tank attachments for five gallon tanks. If you want to use the smaller 1 pound tanks, you will have to purchase an adapter separately.

7. Rocket Stove

Rocket stoves are pretty interesting. Not only could you use it for cooking, but you could use it as a heat source as well. A rocket stove uses small wood fuel which is burned in a simple high-temperature combustion chamber containing a vertical chimney and a secondary air supply which ensures almost complete combustion prior to the flames reaching the cooking surface.

You can purchase these stoves online and the best price I have found was on Amazon for $160.00. Or, if you are handy, you can make one too. Unfortunately, I am not that gifted when it comes to making something like this, so I would rather leave the hard work to someone who really knows what they are doing in constructing something like this.

8. Charcoal Fire Pit

This is easy, and can be created in your backyard. If you are thrifty, you may be able to build this for less than $50.00. Basically a fire pit that you have created by digging a wide fire box area, so dig down about 8 inches, and line the pit with bricks, the floor (base) as well as the walls. Then, around the upper edge, place bricks all around it, lying flat, and do this with two to three rows of brick. And now you have created a pit you can not only cook in using charcoal, but you could use it for a wood fire as well. I like to use charcoal in mine, because it is easy to use, the bricks heat up and help to keep the heat in the deeper 'box', which works great for doing some Dutch Oven cooking in. I like the wide brick base around it to help keep the area well marked, and cleared of debris, so people know this is a fire area. We don't get to use it very often because we have had such a high fire risk lately, but I am happy we made it.

There are other alternatives, such as cooking over an open fire, (which you could do if you have a fire pit in your backyard and you are allowed to do so.) there are alternatives to using electricity to heat your dinner, it's just a matter of using what you have, and using your imagination to figure it out. The best reward though is being able to provide hot meals for your family.

However, if you are in a situation where there is no electricity, and the neighbors are hungry as well, remember you will have to try and disguise your cooking. Which leads to our next area;

Cooking under the Radar

In a situation where there is no electricity, you need to think about the things that would happen after the power went out, and how everyday life would change.

For the first 3 days, it would not be all too horrible, most people do have enough food in their homes that they could make it for 3 days if they had too. Many may not be happy about it, but they would make due, wither with their own food, or that of their neighbors and relatives to make it work. However from the fourth day forward that things would start to unravel a little more quickly.

Although we all should be planning for an extended event of being without electricity, the luxury of having bank cards that work, and a local grocery store many people are not ready for that.

For those that are prudent, and plan ahead by storing food, water, supplies and whatever else they may need will have the added peace of mind that they can, and will be able to provide for themselves and whoever else they were planning on having during a situation like this.

But by having the food, and gas, and all of the necessary supplies you might be a target for those who did not have the foresight to plan ahead.

So let's says the SHTF, and you live in a rural area. Although you are a little freaked out at the situation, you methodically go through your supplies, see what you have, and feel a little bit better because you know you have enough of everything to keep you going for at least 18 months, and by that time your garden will have been harvested, and your baby chicks will producing eggs along with having enough livestock to butcher. Everything will be ok, or so you think.

Now let's say it is the same SHTF scenario, and you live in a more suburban type area, not the city, but the suburbs. You too have been preparing, and have a close knit neighborhood. Your children all attend the same school, and as a group you have been discussing staying more prepared, but you don't want your neighbors to think you are a complete nut job, so you don't show them everything you have be stockpiling throughout your home. Just like the rural prepper, although a little shaken up that the crap has really happened, you feel a small it of relief knowing you will be ok and you will get through this.

And just one more scenario to think about. Same SHTF scenario, but you live in a big city. Although your apartment is small, you too have been stocking up on as much as you can, and finding very creative ways to store your preps. Through your careful planning and calculations, you have enough food water and other supplies to last you about 6 months in case you are not able to leave your apartment home. You also have a small patio which you have become a rather skilled gardener, creating multiple container gardens that you are able to harvest enough fruits and vegetables for your family, some of your neighbors, and even to do some canning, thus adding to your preps.

In each of the above scenarios, the people are well prepared, and have the necessary supplies to get through and extended amount of time if a SHTF scenario were to happen. But something that many preppers forget in their planning...cooking without detection.

Eating is something we all do. Everyone eats out of necessity, some for the sheer joy of eating, others for comfort. No matter how you look at it, we all need to eat. And when we go without food at first we just get hungry, but after you have been hungry for an extended amount of time, hunger can make you do things you wouldn't normally do, or act in a way you wouldn't normally act. This can be intensified in a group, or mob type situation.

So a week or so after the SHTF, people are going to be running out of food, getting desperate to feed their families and looking for food. While they are searching for food certain senses will be heightened. The largest impact will be the sense of smell. So if you are out cooking on your backyard grill, that smell will carry and may bring a lot of attention not only to the meal you are preparing, but also the thought that you probably have more food. Even if you live in a semi-rural or rural area the smell of your cooking will carry very far, in some cases more than ½ a mile away.

So what do you do? You have to eat too. And after all, you and your family were the ones that were planning for this to happen all along. Why should you not be able to cook on your grill or backyard fire pit, right? Well, kind of. If you live in a community of likeminded individuals, or have a very large group of people that can protect your property and your food supply at all times, you may be able to do it. But why take that chance? There are things that you can do to cook incognito, or at least minimize the smells from lingering out to those who have run out of food.

- ### Cook in Bags and Foil

There are cooking bags you can purchase that will hold the yummy aroma inside of whatever it is you are cooking. Nothing is completely scent-proof, but something is better than nothing. You can also wrap whatever it is you are cooking in several layers of aluminum foil. The layers of the foil will help to trap the smell, but won't make it invisible.

- ### Freeze Dried Foods

If you are cooking freeze dried foods, all you have to do is add hot water in many instances, and you will have a hot meal, ready as soon as your water is prepared. This is another reason why it is so important to have an adequate water supply. If you have no electricity and no way to cook other than a fire pit you have created, or your backyard grill, boiling a pot full of water is not going to carry a scent. Boil your water, and then take it inside to create your meal.

- ### Spices

Although spices really add a lot to our cooking, keep the spices for inside. Spices have delicious scents that will make your mouth water even if you aren't starving, think about what it would be like if you hadn't eaten a real meal in a week? Save the spices until you bring your meal to your table inside your home, away from prying eyes, and noses.

o **The Time of Day**

Instead of creating your meals in conventional times of breakfast, lunch and dinner, you may have to alter when you do your outside cooking. Try to do your cooking either late at night or really early in the morning when most people will be sleeping. This is important to keep in mind with the type of cooking you will be doing as well. Remember, flames create light, which could peak interest of those who may be lurking, and along with the light from the fire, if you are cooking during the day the smell of smoke will travel. Keep these things in mind when you are planning your cooking.

o **Cooking Inside Your Home**

If you have the capability to continue to cook inside of your home you still need to pay attention to all of the other points listed above. By keeping your situation as quiet as possible, you will help to keep what you have to yourself. Now that being said, do not, I repeat, DO NOT bring your outdoor grill, charcoal grill or fire pit into your home to cook! Not only do you run the risk of burning your house to the ground, your house will not be ventilated properly to be able to sustain the cooking method. So please, do not bring an outdoor cooking appliance into your home, it just isn't worth the risk.

If you have a wood burning stove and some foil or a Dutch oven, you could cook over your fire. But remember smoke travels, and if during the day someone sees smoke coming from a chimney, you will be announcing to your neighbors "Hey, I have the ability to make fire! My house is warm!" If you make a fire in the dark the smell of the smoke will carry, but it may be a little more challenging to determine which house it is coming from. And if you have done your homework and blacked out your windows so no light is escaping from your home you will be taking one added step to keeping your family safe, and hopefully go undetected.

There are indoor cooking items you can purchase, like a thermal cooker. A thermal cooker is basically a large thermos that you can fit a pot inside (they are sold with the inner pot) so you could start whatever you are creating for your meal outside on the grill or cook stove, and after it reaches a boiling temperature for about 10 minutes, bring it inside, add your other ingredients, and put the pot with the lid inside of the thermal container. It will continue to cook for 6-8 hours, it is completely sealed so the smell won't permeate your home, or outside, and you can have a hot filling dinner, without anyone being the wiser.

If you have the luxury of a generator, making you able to heat your home, run the lights, and your appliances, consider yourself very luck, and a target. If you are using a gas generator, that sound will carry, possibly making your home a target for those who are not as fortunate as you. If you can, instead of investing in a gas generator, consider investing in a solar one. A solar generator is quiet, and you would be able to hide or camouflage it if you had too. If you live in an environment that gets a lot of sunny days, buy the solar generator. Even if it's a small one, you could charge it during the day, and bring it inside at night, plug in a hotplate and cook up a can of stew or chili.

o **Garbage**

Having left overs of previous meals, and the trash can alert others to what you have. Try to keep your meals small, so there is no food to go to waste. Also scraps could be made useful in other areas, including compost or pet food, depending on what you are eating for that meal. Almost everything we consume can be reused in one way or another. Cardboard boxes can be used in composting, or for fire starting. Large metal cans can be used to create candle holders, or even hobo stoves. So strive to have minimal waste or trash. Home recycle what you can (by reusing or repurposing) There won't be any trash service, and waste that is left lying around can invite pests, which in turn can bring in bacteria, and sickness. If you do have trash that you cannot reuse or repurpose have a designated area that the trash can be buried or burnt. But don't let the garbage pile up.

These examples are just a few to keep in mind when considering how you are going to be able to cook after the SHTF. These aren't just things to think about, but things you can and should be practicing now. By learning different skills, not only are you preparing your skills, but you are making yourself a valuable asset for your family or your group. Play with the ideas, try cooking outside in foil, and see how far away the scent travels. Try alternative cooking methods, like a Dutch oven, a solar oven, or creating a fire pit. If you have a wood burning stove insert or free standing, cook on top of it, and even inside. Practice makes perfect, and the more practice you have, the better you will become not only with your cooking, but also your ability to camouflage your cooking.

In times of need, you have options. Keep that in mind if you are presented with an emergency situation. The more you practice these alternative methods, the better prepared you will be when an actually emergency is thrown in your face.

It is a good idea to have at least three different ways to prepare meals for your family. If that means your stove is one, your grill is another, what is your third? Try the options we have listed here for you, and become proficient in as many different ways to cook as possible.

CANNING

So you have successfully been able to grow vegetables and fruit from your gardening efforts (which will be described in a later chapter. Sorry this book doesn't go in order, but C does come before G, so you get to learn how to preserve your bounty before you grow it!) Or, you have gotten a killer deal on tomatoes corn, or whatever it is that you found at a great price that you couldn't pass up.

But those fresh fruits and veggies won't last forever, so how will you preserve them? Canning food offers long term food storage for the food you have been able to grow. Just think, by canning your food, you will be able to enjoy the corn you grew last summer into the coldness of winter.

Canning isn't difficult, as long as you follow some simple rules. When you can food, it must be heated to a certain temperature. At the certain temperature, food spoiling bacteria are killed. The heat also forces air to leave the jar. As the jar cools, it will create a seal and no bacteria will be able to enter the jar. With this type of preservation, canned food can last for many years.

Canning food can seem scary, and intimidating. We have all heard stories of people who have died from botulism from eating home canned food. And although this is probably true, it doesn't have to leave you thinking canning is dangerous or scary.

The USDA has created guidelines that if followed, will produce safe food that can be eaten years later. You can Google USDA Canning guidelines, and print off the information. I find it handy to have the guidelines open while I am canning. If anything for peace of mind, but I will read and re-read the instructions at least four times while my jars are boiling. Not only does the USDA give precise times, there are hundreds of recipes. If you have the fruit and vegetables, you will be able to create a vast assortment of canned treasures!

There are two methods of canning, boiling water bath, and a pressure canner, using steam. The type of food you want to can, will determine which method you will be using. This is further determined by the level of acidity the food has. The lower the acidity, the longer organisms, such as bacteria will survive at a given temperature. So less acidic foods are canned with a pressure canner, because the temperature rises to 240 degrees Fahrenheit. The types of food that you will use a pressure canner for are vegetables, meat and poultry.

By going to the USDA website, and look up home canning, you will find eight different links that will open up pdf files. You can download these to your computer, or print them off. I find it the best to print them off, and place them in a binder and keep it as a reference guide for canning, you will be very happy you did.

There is so much information available about canning from the USDA site, over one hundred pages of canning, recipes, and procedures. I could put it here, but I would rather direct you to the site so you can find what you like, and use it.

The equipment you will need for canning:

- o Boiling -Water Canner
- o Pressure Canner
- o Canning Jars
- o Lids and Bands
- o Canning Salt (not table salt)
- o The fruits, vegetables, and meats you want to can (but it is best to do one item at a time, believe me I learned this from trying to do too much in a weekend!)

And keep in mind once your food has been canned effectively, and safely, it will last pretty much forever. I don't know how appetizing a twenty year old jar of spaghetti sauce maybe, but if I were hungry enough, I bet I would find out.

When you have canned your food items, they should be stored in an area that is dark, and moisture free. By keeping your canned jars in a temperate environment, you help to make sure the jars stay sealed. Moisture is also a consideration. You don't want to store your jars in a moist environment because this could damage your seals. If your jars are sealed, and you canned them following the appropriate instructions for whatever items you are canning, and no oxygen was able to get into your jars, they should last a very long time.

And that is what this is all about, being prepared, and making the most of what you have. If canning is a viable option for your family, you should at least consider it wouldn't you agree?

Water Bath Canning

The Boiling water, or water bath, canner is for more acidic foods, such as fruits, jams and jellies. These foods have a pH of less than 4.6. The USDA guide gives specific times of how long the food must be boiled. Make sure you follow the instructions to ensure your canned food is safe to eat.

Foods that can be water bath canned are:

- Fruits
- Pickles
- Jams or Jellies
- Sauerkraut
- Tomatoes (with the addition of lemon juice or citric acid)

Tips to keep in mind when using a water bath canner:

1. Make sure your jars are in good condition. They don't have to be new, but they do have to be in good shape. If there are nicks in the glass, the jar could crack, and if there are nicks or chips in the rim, you will not get a good seal. So make sure all of your glass jars are in excellent condition.
2. Have a very large area in which to can. Canning takes a lot of space, and can be messy. The more room you have the better.
3. Give yourself extra time. Undoubtedly, the first time you plan on canning it will take extra time. So give yourself the time you will need, especially the first few times you are canning. Every time you do it you will get faster and more efficient. But in the beginning, give yourself a lot of extra time.
4. Follow the directions. When it comes to canning creativity is not a good plan. This is food you are preparing and will be storing long term. Do yourself a favor, and follow the directions explicitly. You do not want to mess with the safety of your food, because it could have very bad consequences. Save your creative side for your regular recipes, not your canning.

5. Start small. Try not to get ahead of yourself. For your first canning experience, stick with 1 item you will be canning, like pickles, or jam. Start with 6 quart jars, and when you have mastered that, then move up to larger projects. But it is a good idea to stick with 1 item at a time.

Pressure Canning

The pressure canner is used for vegetables, meats, and anything with a pH over 4.6. This is where you have to be careful, and pay attention to the temperatures and the timing depending on what type of food you are canning. You can find canning guidelines easily on the internet. And the websites that I have used have been listed in the resources section of this book.

Pressure canners are more expensive than water bath canners, but they are highly specialized pieces of equipment. When you can with pressure, the heat inside of the canner builds up, under pressure. This allows the temperature to rise higher than it can in a water bath canner.

One thing to keep in mind when you are canning with a pressure canner is your stove. If you have a stove that is gas, or has a regular heating element, you will be fine no matter what type of canning you will be doing. However, if you have a glass top stove, check with the manufacture of your stove to make sure it can withstand the rigors of canning.

Making the jump from water bath canning to pressure caning can seem a little daunting, but it doesn't have to be. For the best instructions, it is best to use a trusted guide. The very best I have found, and use is The Ball Blue Book Guide to Preserving. This is a must have for your canning adventure whether it is water bath canning, or pressure canning.

Pressure Canning does not have to be intimidating. We all have heard stories of pressure canners blowing up, or the food spoiling because the canning was not done correctly. But pressure canners have changed a lot since they were first introduced.

The main difference between water bath canning and pressure canning is the temperature, and the types of food you will be preserving. With pressure canning you are preserving food that has a pH higher than 4.6. You can also preserve acidic foods with a pressure canner, which makes this type of food preservation more versatile, so if you have to choose one type of canning system, this would probably be the wiser investment.

Like everything, when you decide you want to preserve your own food, make sure you do your homework. The first time will not be easy, and it will take a lot longer than you anticipated, so plan for it. But with practice, you will become proficient in your skills, and the time it takes you to preserve food will drastically cut down.

Foods that typically require pressure canning or those with a higher pH level, or low acid level, however you choose to look at it. But the foods that must be pressure canned are:

- o Meats
- o Seafood
- o Poultry
- o Vegetables
- o Complete Meals (like soup, stews and sauces)

I have heard you can preserve dairy products as well, however I choose to buy dried powdered type dairy products because of the cost and ease of use. The Ball canning guide is an excellent resource for specifics, as is the USDA website.

The benefit to the USDA website is it is free, and if you have any concerns or questions about any type of canning, you will find it there. They are PDF files that are easily printed out, and you can store them in a binder for a reference. Just as an example, the first PDF is 40 pages long, but there is SO much information! In total, there are 7 "guides" that you can either download or print. I chose to print them, and add them to my library. A total book (or binder) of all of the guides once printed is 182 valuable pages of home canning information and recipes galore!

Once I was able to print all of the pages, I made a dedicated binder for my canning information, and it lives in my kitchen with a few of my other favorite cookbooks. For the reference sheets, I used packing tape on them to seal them so if I do spill something on the paper, it will not be ruined. (I have done this with my favorite recipes as well)

Dry Canning

You may not consider dry canning to be 'real' canning, but if it comes to food that is stored in a jar for long term food storage, I would consider this a very viable, and simple option for food storage. The added benefit is that you aren't required to use a water bath canner or pressure canner. Dry canning is simply creating shelf-stable meals in sealed jars that you just add a few ingredients too, and presto, you have a meal.

You have probably seen the recipes as jar recipes, for things such as soups, stews and cookies. You layer the ingredients into the jar, dress them up with a bow, and you have a beautiful homemade gift to give at any time of the year. But I decided I don't want to just have gifts to give, but I wanted to be able to have these meals for my own family, call me selfish, but I want to make sure I have lots of options for my family when it comes to easy to prepare meals.

It is really easy to create a meal out of things you already have in your food storage pantry, and there are many websites that have hundreds of jar recipes that you can customize to your own liking. After you have added all of your ingredients to the jar, you simply place an oxygen absorber on the top, seal the jar and place with your other jars. And wha-la! You have added meals to your food storage that will last for years! And, even though it isn't a requirement or even necessary, the jars will look will pretty on your shelf.

Here is an easy recipe that I have modified a little bit from everyone's favorite, chocolate chip cookies.

Country Girl Chocolate Chip Cookies

Create fantastic cookies chock full of chocolate chips and tasty pecans in just a couple of minutes with this delicious Country girl chocolate chip cookies a jar.

You'll Need:

1 1/3 cups quick oats

1/2 cup firmly packed brown sugar

1/2 cup sugar

1/2 cup chopped pecans

1/2 cup milk chocolate chips

1/2 cup mini semisweet chocolate chips

1 1/3 cups flour

1 teaspoon baking powder

1 teaspoon baking soda

1/4 teaspoon salt

Measure each item into layers if giving as a jar gift. The above list makes 1 complete Jar or 1 Package of mix. Before putting lid on your jar, put 1 oxygen absorber on top of the ingredients prior to closing the jar.

Recipe Tag Directions:

Combine the following until well blended:

1 Jar of mix

1 stick butter melted

1 egg slightly beaten

1 tsp vanilla

Shape into small balls the size of walnuts place 2 inches apart on sprayed baking sheets.

Bake at 350°F for 11 to 13 minutes until edges are lightly browned.

And here is another simple recipe for a meal

Beef Chili Mix

1/2 cup dried red kidney beans

1/2 cup dried navy beans

1/2 cup dried black beans

1/3 cup dried minced onions

2 to 3 tablespoons chili powder

2 tablespoons dried cilantro or parsley flakes

2 teaspoons ground cumin

1 teaspoon salt

1/2 teaspoon dried minced garlic

Layer all ingredients in a quart wide mouth jar, and put an oxygen absorber on top of ingredients, seal the jar and attach a tag with directions.

Attach Tag:

In a Dutch oven, brown 2 pounds ground beef; drain. Add ingredients from the jar, plus 6 cups water; bring to a boil, reduce heat, cover and simmer for 1 1/2 to 2 hours, until beans are tender. Or you can put everything in a crockpot on high for 3 hours, and then turn down to low for about 6 hours.

Add 3 (14 1/2 ounce) cans tomato juice. Bring to a boil; reduce heat, cover and simmer for 15 minutes.

8 servings

It doesn't matter if you choose dry canning, water bath canning or pressure canning, whichever route you decide to try will be what works best for you. Keep in mind the most important part is to try. You will never know what you are capable of if you don't try it, so make a promise to yourself to try canning something at least once.

CHICKENS

I have to tell you, chickens are one of my favorite aspects of being more self-reliant. These little animals are a wonderful addition to our family, as I am sure they would be to yours as well. Chickens serve as a renewable source. They eat relatively little, and give so much in return. A chicken can produce eggs, and also provide meat for your family. Chickens are entertaining, and they are a very important part of providing food. They require very little upkeep, and if you are just getting started with producing some of your own food, they are a great way to get started. But make sure to check into your local laws, ordinances, and HOA rules. For example, our subdivision, we are allowed chickens, but no roosters. So unfortunately the little chicks we buy, if they end up being a boy they will become dinner for our family later on.

The easiest way to get started with chicken raising is by going to your local feed store in the early spring. They will usually have some that are "sexed" (meaning if they are male or female). If there are no feed stores within your local area, baby chicks can be purchased online, and shipped to you through the mail. I haven't gone that route yet, but whatever it takes to get you started is what counts.

When you decide to buy chickens, planning your purchase first before you bring the babies home will be less stressful for you and them. Trust me, it can be exciting, but if you are running around the store picking up the things you think you will need, and getting the chicks at the same time, you will be running around trying to make sure everything is perfect for them. This will be stressful for you and the chicks. So plan a trip to the feed store to buy what you will need BEFORE you bring the chicks home.

If you aren't quite sure if chickens are for you, read up online or go to the library and check out a few books of what it really needed to raise chickens. If it seems like something you can picture yourself doing, start off small. Start with 2 to 3 chicks until you get the hang of it, because at first those baby chicks will need to stay warm, so unless you have a heated barn and special incubation system for your chicks, they will probably be living in your home until they are big enough to go outside into their own house.

Starting chickens from chicks is not difficult, and they are very forgiving, as long as you remember to keep them warm, feed them, water them, and keep their box or pen clean. So let's keep this simple, and start with what your baby chicks will need from the time you bring them home.

The things you will need to get started with chicks:

- A large box or storage container (I use a clear Rubbermaid tote)
- A screen to put on top of the container (we use a portion of a dog kennel
- A heat light
- A water source
- A 2" brick to set the waterer on
- A chick size feeder
- Pine shavings
- Medicated chick feed
- Electrolyte solution
- Chick grit

And that's it! Well, you still need your baby chicks, but wait to buy them until you get their new home set up. Once you bring your baby chicks home, you will need to monitor their housing, the temperature, their food and water, and cleanliness. Baby chicks should be kept indoors until they have their all of their feathers, which happens when they are about 8 to 12 weeks old.

Once you have their home ready, it is now time to get your chicks. You can purchase them online, but if you do have a local feed or farm store where you can purchase them, this is the best option if you are just starting out. I say this for two reasons. One, the chicks will be a little bit older, and thus a little easier to care for if they are a couple of weeks old. You won't have to worry as much about them having problems with 'pasting' (this is where their poop gets matted onto their tiny rear ends, and then they can die) and two, the feed store that is selling the baby chicks know what type of chickens will thrive in your local area. What do I mean by this you may be wondering? But certain chickens will do better in certain areas. For example, where we live the elevation is high, and certain breeds of chickens cannot tolerate the altitude. We need hardy breeds that are lighter, and sometimes crossbred chickens work well too. I'm not going to go into breeds of chickens, there are many other books that do a fantastic job of that.

So that is the basics of what you need for chicks, and continue reading for a little more in depth on each area of raising your chicks.

The Chick Brooder

Your chicks first home is called a brooder. For one-time or once-in-a-while use, a cardboard box works ok, but I prefer to use a large clear plastic storage container. I find for multiple uses and planning on having baby chicks each spring, the clear plastic tub works even better. You can use a cage like you would use for a guinea pig or a rabbit and it's easy to clean.

 Hopefully you can see by these examples, basically anything that is like a box will work for your chicks for their first home. We keep the top open, and when the chicks get big enough to start "flying", we take a piece of dog kennel and use it as a grate to keep them in their home. We have also used old window screens to keep the chicks in their home, but making it so there is plenty of air circulation.

No matter what type of 'home' you choose, the bottom should have a layer of clean pine shavings or newspaper. This will be the 'litter' for the chicks.

Newspaper print ink can get the chicks dirty though, so we've never used it, and it can also be slippery. The litter should be changed out every couple of days, and never allowed to remain damp. Cleanliness is VERY important at this stage of your baby chickens lives. Baby chicks are prone to a number of diseases, most of which can be avoided by keeping their home clean and dry.

The size of the brooder depends on how many chicks you have. The chicks should have enough room to move around, and to lay down and sleep. You will also need to have enough space in the brooder for a waterer and a feeder.

Temperature

The brooder can be heated by using a light bulb with a reflector. These are readily available at hardware and feed stores. A 100-watt bulb is usually good, though some prefer to use an actual heat lamp. I have tried the heat lamp and found that with the type of brooder I use (a large plastic tote) It gets too hot with the heat lamp, so I prefer the regular 100-watt bulb. The temperature should be 90-100 degrees for the first week or so, then can be reduced by 5 degrees each week thereafter, until the chicks have their feathers, when they are about 5 to 8 weeks old.

A thermometer in the brooder is helpful, but you can tell if the temperature is right by how the chicks behave. If they are panting and/or huddling in corners farthest from the light, they are too hot. If they huddle together in a ball under the light, they are too cold. You can adjust the distance of the light (or change the wattage of the bulb) until the temperature is just right. This is a balancing act, and requires a lot of monitoring on your part, but trust me, it will be worth it in just a few short months.

Water

Clean, fresh water must always be available to your chicks. Get at least a medium size waterer because chicks drink a lot of water. I like this plastic kind because it's easy to clean, inexpensive, lightweight and they can't tip it over.

Your chicks will also poop everywhere, including right into their water. One way that I have found to tackle this problem is to raise the waterer so that it is difficult for them to get into it. Just make sure they can still get to the water. You should plan on cleaning the waterer at least once a day and depending on how crowded it is, even twice a day is not a bad idea.

When the chicks are about a month old, you can add a low roost - a stick or piece of wood dowelling about 4" off the floor of the brooder. The chicks will jump on it and may even begin sleeping there. But don't put the roost directly under the light because it will be too hot.

Feeders and Feeding

Even baby chicks will naturally scratch at their food, so a feeder that (more or less) keeps the food in one place is good. You can find chick feeders online or at the store where you bought your chicks. There will usually be a top that you can remove to fill the feeder. Again, cleanliness is important; the chicks will poop right into their own food, so you must clean and refill it often.

Chicks start out with food called crumbles. It is specially formulated for their dietary needs. You can buy medicated feed, or unmedicated feed. I don't like to take risks, so I have always bought the medicated feed. If you don't use medicated feed, you run the risk that Coccidiosis will infect and wipe out as much as 90% of your chicks. Coccidiosis is a parasitic disease of the intestinal tract of animals caused by coccidian protozoa. The disease spreads from one animal to another by contact with infected feces or ingestion of infected tissue. Diarrhea, which may become bloody in severe cases, is the primary symptom. This is why I choose to use a medicated chick feed, I love my little chicks, and I would hate for something like this to happen.

The feed is a complete food - no other food is necessary. However, feeding your chicks treats can be fun. After the first week or two, you can give them a worm or a bug or two from your garden to play with and eat. Greens like lettuce and grass is not a good idea for young chicks because they can cause diarrhea-like symptoms. When droppings are loose, a condition may develop called "pasting up", where droppings stick to the vent area and harden up, preventing the chick from eliminating. Check the chicks for pasting often - if you see this, clean off the vent area, their butt, you can use a moist towel or even some mineral oil if you are having difficulty getting them clean.

Playing with You Chicks

Chicks are incredibly curious. After the weather gets warmer, they can be put outside for short periods of time if they are old enough, we will take our babies' outside to 'play' when they are about four weeks old. They must be watched closely at this age, however. Chicks can move fast, squeeze into small spaces, and are helpless against a variety of predators, including the family dog or cat. If they have bonded to you (the first large thing a baby chicks sees is forever it's 'mama', this is called "imprinting"), they will follow you around. Chickens become affectionate of their owners. Some will come when you call them, and some won't, so don't take it personally.

Once your chicks have their feathers, and if the weather is warm, you can start planning on moving them to their permanent home outside.

Chicken Coops

Once the babies have their feathers, it's time to start thinking about moving them outside permanently. When you start planning to move them outside into a chicken coop keep in mind that it takes about 3 to 4 square feet per chicken inside the henhouse and 10 sq/ft per chicken in an outside run. Also, don't forget about your local chicken predators, and make a safe home for your flock.

You can buy a ready-made chicken coop, but they can be

really expensive. As long as your chickens have a nice dry place to rest and roost, and get some outside time, they will be pretty happy. You can make a coop from an old storage shed, or a few sheets of plywood. Just make sure your hens have laying boxes for laying their eggs. You can take crates and lay them with the opening on the side, put some straw in it, and voila! You have a nesting box!

When it comes to building a home for your chickens, you are only limited by your imagination, and carpentry skills. Your chickens will be happy if they are able to stay warm and dry, and they really aren't very picky past that.

Bedding

 Pine shavings work really well in the summer and if you live in a warm climate, and they can be a part of your garden compost too. In our hen house, we fill the entire house with straw during the winter. And then when I clean out the house, I transfer all of the used bedding out to my compost pile. So the bedding serves two purposes, it provides a comfortable surface for the chickens when it is new, and once it is no longer functional for bedding purposes, it helps to add dead material to the compost bed.

Temperature

Depending on what area you live in, you will need to make sure your chickens are comfortable in both the hottest times of the year as well as the coldest. During the summer, make sure they have a shaded area in order to stay cool. Keep their waterers full, and in the heat of summer, we like to add a few ice cubes to their water.

And when the weather turns colder, you will also need to

make sure they are able to stay warm, and that their water source does not freeze. I personally use a heated plastic waterer, and although not a perfect solution, (They don't seem to last that long, maybe a year or two.) the heated waterer serves the purpose of making sure the chickens are able to have access to water at all times.

Food & Water

There are so many different types of commercial chicken feed layer feed or pellets. My chickens seem to do really well with the same "crumble" type of food they had when they were chicks, so that's what I use. Right now I can buy a bag of feed for about $14.00. This will last us about two months for our small flock of six chickens. In return they give us at least a dozen eggs a week, and all of the fertilizer we could possible need for our garden. I would call that a fair trade. You can also free range your chickens if you have a large area for them, and they will probably do very well with a little food added to supplement their diet, and to make sure they are getting what they need.

You can buy feeders and waters, or you can repurpose old bowls and even pie plates. In the winter we have purchased a heated waterer, because the chickens always need to have access to clean water.

Treats

Vegetables, bread, bugs, chicken scratch (cracked corn, milo, wheat) there is pretty much no wrong thing you can feed to your chickens as a treat. Instead of throwing out vegetables, we regularly feed the leftovers to our chickens, and they love it! You do need to be careful too though, just like dogs, chickens can't digest chocolate, so the treats you like to eat, like sugary snacks and junk food, keep them away from your chickens.

The best thing about chickens is that they are very easy to maintain, and are very forgiving, which is why they make a great starting point if you are just starting to venture into a more self-reliant or prepping lifestyle.

Caring for the Eggs

Before we get into the major reason many of us want chickens, I feel it is really important to remind everyone to always wash your hands with soap and water after handling eggs, chickens, or anything in their environment.

Ok, now for the fun part! This is where you really get the benefit of having your own flock of chickens, their eggs!

When your chickens begin laying eggs, all of the work you have done to get them raised to this point will be rewarded. Your hens should start laying eggs when the reach about 6-8 months of age. Some will lay sooner, some later. But in general, the age they begin laying is about 6 months old. But the age of the chicken is not the only factor to consider for egg laying. You will also need to have enough daylight hours for your hens to begin laying. In the longer hours of the spring and summer, egg production will be about 1 egg per day per hen. But that will slow down in the winter when there is less daylight, and also when the hens molt. You can 'encourage' wintertime egg production by adding lights and making your girls think it's still summer time, and they should be in egg production mode. That is up to you, but we choose to let nature take its course, and we don't get to upset if our chickens are not laying eggs year round. We get enough eggs from our flock to not only provide eggs for our family, but also about three families that I work with.

Make sure to collect the eggs often. Eggs that spend more time in the nest have an increased chance of becoming dirty, broken, or lower in quality. Collecting eggs at least twice daily is a good idea. Depending on how big your flock is, you may want to consider a third collection in late afternoon or early evening, especially in hot or cold weather. Keep old coffee cans, or pails in order to make your egg collection easier. Also it is safer to discard eggs with broken or cracked shells.

Dirty eggs can be a health hazard. Eggs with dirt and debris can be cleaned pretty easily. You don't have to get fancy when you are cleaning your eggs. We like to use a dish scrubber that has the soap in the handle. We only use this for the eggs, but it is easy to run the water in the sink, and scrub the debris from the eggs, rinse them off and then set them on a towel to dry. Even if the eggs look clean, we still always wash them. I mean think about it, where do the eggs come from??? When washing your eggs, the temperature of the water should be at least 20F warmer than the egg. This will prevent the egg contents from contracting and producing a vacuum. It will also prevent microscopic bacteria from being pulled by vacuum through the pores of the egg. A mild, non-foaming, unscented detergent approved for washing eggs can be used, which is why I use dishwashing liquid soap. If you are still concerned about the safety of your eggs, you can sanitize them by dipping in a solution of 1 tablespoon household bleach to 1 gallon of water before storage.

Dry your eggs before storing because moisture may enter the shell pores as eggs cool on refrigeration.

Store eggs in the main section of the refrigerator at 35F to 40F; the shelves in the door tend to be warmer than interior shelves. If collected and stored properly, eggs can have a safe shelf life of greater than three weeks. Date the storage carton or container and use older eggs first. If you have more eggs than you can use, you can break them out of their shells and freeze them. You should only freeze fresh eggs. Beat until just blended, pour into freezer containers, seal tightly, label with the number of eggs and the date. If you want to get fancy, you can add a small amount of salt, sugar, or other spices to improve the keeping quality of the eggs. Make sure to label any additional ingredients on the freezer container. If you are feeling really creative, you can freeze the egg whites and yolks separately.

Another aspect of having chickens is they can provide meat for your family. This isn't a bad thing when you think about it. I mean you go to the store and buy chicken all the time. If you raise your own chickens to butcher, the best piece of advice I can give you is to remember what the chickens are there for. They are there to feed your family, and yes, you will have to kill them, however, the chickens (probably roosters) will have had a much better life in your small coop than if they were raised for their meat at a chicken farm.

Chickens that are raised for meat by corporations don't really get a chance at having a decent life.

This is no way for animals to live. But this is how chickens spend their lives when they are produced by the millions. So instead of having a live in a small cage, when you raise your own chickens they have a life, and are able to run around and be chickens.

And I also feel it is important for myself, and my family to know where our food comes from. And although butchering the chickens isn't my favorite part, in order to have food it needs to be done. I feel it gives me a respect for the food I have, and also I understand where my food comes from.

Butchering chickens isn't for everyone, and if you choose to only have hens that's great! You are taking one step closer to being more self-reliant, and living more responsibly. I am not going to get into the actual deed of butchering and processing chickens here. There are many books and even videos available to watch on YouTube that walk you through the process. This is actually how we learned how to do it for the first time. It isn't glamorous, or something I would like to do every day, but I know how to do it now, so when it has to be done, I can do it. I hope one day you can say the same thing.

Although butchering and processing chickens is a harder topic to end this chapter on, it is a very important aspect of being more self-reliant and growing your own food. Now that you know a little more about chickens, I advise you to map out your plan for getting chickens and getting started with raising them. The more information you have, and the more you prepare for, the better of you and your family will be. So now it's time to get out there and get your own chickens!

COMPOST

One of the most important aspects of growing food, or creating beautiful landscapes is having good soil in which a plant can grow. I am sure you have seen beautiful parks, and flowerbeds or admired gorgeous gardens on websites and wondered how they do it. It does take a lot of work, years of practice and tinkering, but the results are so worth it. But, how do you get that amazing garden, or flower bed? How can you grow huge vegetables? The easiest answer is good soil, and that comes from compost.

Composting is an integral part of gardening. In order for anything we plant, we need to have a good foundation (soil) that provides nutrients that will help aid your plants to grow to their fullest potential.

The best way that I have found to do this is through composting. Composting is when you take dirt, organic material, meaning dead material and living organisms to create the black gold (good soil) to act as a soil amendment, and also to provide nutrients naturally instead of relying on fertilizer to get the job done. Personally I like to use "natural" fertilizers instead of commercially produced because it's cheaper, better for my garden, and better for the food I am producing for myself and my family.

Compost can be looked at through scientific eyes, and learning all the components of the soil, the bacteria, the nutrients, and many microorganisms. When fertilizers and hybrid seeds are used, the soil loses. And with each subsequent planting and using chemicals, the soil continues to be depleted of everything natural. This makes it more and more difficult to grow food naturally, and requires more and more chemicals and commercial fertilizers in order to grow anything. If we can incorporate more natural and relatively simple ideas back into our gardening not only are we going to have larger yields, but we will be putting nutrients and microorganisms back into the ground, where we really need them to be.

Making compost isn't difficult, but it does take time. You don't have to have the fancy compost turners or bins, a raised bed will work just fine for creating compost. Or, if you just have a dedicated area, which will be used for composting, this can work too. Like with anything, you have to get out there and do it to determine what is going to work best for you and your garden.

To get started, designate an area that you can use for composting. The picture below shows a garden bed that has been used multiple times, and I am rebuilding the bed by adding material for composting.

This is the bed in its raw state, nothing has been done, not even the weeds pulled out. I want to show you how easy this is! Don't make it hard! I am starting with just some dirt, just plain dirt that was a part of the original bed.

Then I am going to add my first layer for compost. Since we have an abundance of animals, we have an abundance of manure which can create the first layer. I use rabbit, chicken, and horse poop. The animals make the manure, so I am going to use it!

I will add enough manure to cover the entire bed, about 3 inches, and I spread it out evenly across the bed making sure all of the edges are covered, and filled.

The next layer is the layer of "dead" organic material. Since I use straw in my horses' stalls during the winter, it is already mixed in with some of the manure I have spread into the lower layer of my compost. I add a little extra along with some shredded paper, chopped up cardboard and dried leaves.

The next layer is easy, another layer of dirt. Continue to pile the layers, until it is almost over the sides of the bed. Make the layers like a mound

And this is what your bed will look like when it's ready to just sit. After you have done the layers, soak the bed, and leave it alone. Once a week, you can add some water. Don't allow the water to pool or overfill the area, but saturate it. Continue to keep it damp, and if you want to speed up the process, you can cover it with a heavy plastic tarp. If you are starting your compost in the late fall, early winter, the tarp will help to keep the heat in, which can help to speed up the composting process.

Every 3 to 4 weeks, take a pitchfork or shovel and turn the layers eventually the layers will decompose and in about 4 months or so, you will have compost that is ready to use. If you start this in late fall, depending on what part of the country you live in, your compost will be ready to use by spring. If you keep this up for several years, you will have amazing garden soil. It doesn't happen overnight, and yes, it will take work. However, just like everything you have been working on thus far, it is well worth it.

Now if you are creating your compost in the spring or summer, you can also speed up the decomposition process of your compost by adding living organisms. If you live in a temperate climate, you can do this year round as well. The living organisms will break down the organic material

Black Soldier Flies and Their Larva

Black soldier flies are a wonderful addition to your compost pile. They don't really look like a fly, in fact they kind of resemble a wasp. These little creatures spend most of their lives in the larva stage. This is great news for your compost pile. Not only do the larva have voracious appetites for garbage, but they make quick work of it. They will eat any kind of decaying organic material. They also turn the manure into a more liquid type of material, making the manure unattractive to 'pest' flies such as horse flies and horse flies.

The adults don't live very long, the adult lifespan is about 5 to 8 days. But for every mating, the adult female can produce about 500 eggs that will become larva, and start the lifecycle all over again. They thrive in manure and organic compost, so if you have manure, and organic compost you will be set, and very happy with the work these little can creatures do.

You can try to attract female wild black soldier flies by putting out a food source that they are attracted to, such as fermented fruits and corn. It is also a good idea to have some cardboard lying around throughout your compost area, because the females like to lay their eggs in material.
If you aren't able to entice the black soldier flies to your compost pile, you can purchase the larva online. There are many different places to purchase the larva from, and you may be able to find them locally as well.
As an added bonus, the larva are really high in protein, and can make a great snack for your chickens! But, they are even better for helping with your compost, and helping to breakdown waste. But depending on what part of the world you live, black soldier flies may not naturally inhabit your area because of cold temperatures. You can purchase them online, so if they are not native to your area, you could always try them for a growing season, and then turn your chickens loose in your compost pile when it gets cool. The girls would have a wonderful time searching for the larva, and they would be working your compost at the same time.

Worms

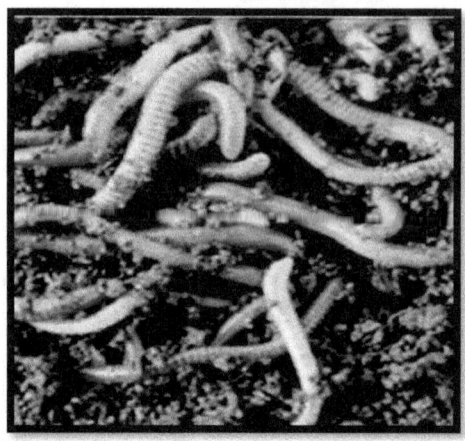

I remember growing up, my mom would always tell me if we had worms in the garden, then it was good ground for growing. I know there is some truth to that, but not sure if it was because of the compost that she added in, or if it were really true. But the fact is, worms are good for your garden, and great for making compost.

There are thousands of different worms you can find, and many you can purchase. The best ones to purchase online are the red wigglers. Red wigglers are small worms that can reach an average length of about 4 inches long. They are great for composting because of their appetites. These little worms can eat their own weight every day! So they will help to devour waste, and create worm manure (castings). These castings are wonderful for your garden.

The worms can be put directly into your compost pile, or you can have a 'worm factory' which is a fancy composting bin for your worms. This may be a good idea if you live in a very cold climate which would allow you to move your worms indoors for the winter. However, I have had good results by just putting the worms directly into my composting area.

But you may be wondering what do you feed your worms in

order to produce fertilizer for your garden? In general, the red wiggler worms will consume fruits and vegetable scraps as well as fruit, left over vegetable scraps and peelings, coffee grounds, tea leaves and tea bags, vacuum cleaner dust (but don't use carpet fresh!), hair clippings (people and animals), manures, shredded paper like newspaper, and crushed egg shells. The greater your variety of material used, the better the compost will be.

So not only are your worms and black soldier flies helping to breakdown garbage, but you are also getting the added benefit of having amazing healthy and fertile garden soil. By adding worms and black soldier flies to your composting, you will be helping to eliminate your own garbage too.

Compost Tea

Yes, you read that correctly...a tea made from compost! Compost tea is full of nutrients and beneficial bacteria that help to fertilize your plants, and can even protect them against fungal diseases. It is pretty simple to make, and doesn't require you to buy any fancy equipment. You can make compost tea in your own backyard. This is how you do it.

What you will need:
10 lbs of mature compost
20 gallons of water
40 gallon trash can
4-5 foot long stick

Directions:
Place the trash can in an area that is protected from extreme heat and cold.
Put the compost into the trash can. I prefer to use a plastic trash can, because I want to make sure the water will not leak out.
Fill the trash can with water.

Stir with a stick daily for at least 6 days. The tea should not smell bad, meaning stinky.

Strain the liquid from the solid material, and use the liquid immediately.

There can be E.Coli in the raw components of compost, so do not use compost tea on vegetables that you will be harvesting within 4 weeks. By using mature compost, you reduce the risk of E.Coli, but the chance is still there. That's why when I make and use compost tea, I like to do it after I first establish my plants, and also use it in the spring around my fruit trees.

Hopefully this gives you a basic idea of composting, and the many benefits it can give you for your own garden. The dirt in which we plant our food is full of life, and in order to grow crops, we need to keep the natural balance, and replace the nutrients that we end up removing from the soil. With compost, you can 'give back' to the soil. And remember, composting isn't hard, and it can save you money while giving something back to the land which we all desperately need to make sure stays healthy. You can start off small, and increase the size of your composting as your skills develop. By learning how to compost and incorporate it into your gardening you will be helping to not only ensure a better harvest this year, but for every year after that as well.

CHECKLISTS

Prepping Checklists

If you have just started down the road to becoming more prepared you may be feeling a little overwhelmed, and a lot under prepared. Wondering where do you even begin. There are so many websites and books telling you to store a year's worth of food in your pantry, but make sure you rotate it, and make sure you plan for short term and long term storage. And you will need to remember your guns, and don't forget alternative power sources, and have at least 20 different weapons, oh and don't forget to store a thousand gallons of water...and...and...and...

First Things First...How Much Money Do You REALLY Spend?

The first place you really should start is looking at your monthly budget so you will know how much you can afford to spend on your prepping. And while you are looking at your budget, figuring out how to get yourself out of debt would be the best place to start. By eliminating your debt, you will not only be giving yourself more money that you can use for prepping, but you will be giving yourself peace of mind. Think about it, many of us have a lot of debt that we don't really need to have. You don't need 5 credit cards. You don't need 3 cars. You don't need to have every single cable channel. You don't need to go out to lunch every single day. By eliminating these debts, you will be giving yourself a freedom you never knew you could have.

So the first part of this is determining how much money you spend on a monthly basis. Grab a spiral notebook, and for the next 30 days, you are going to write down every single time you spend money. I don't care what it is. If you buy groceries on Monday, write it down. If you pay your bills on Tuesday, write it down. Every time you run out to the store, or buy that soda, write it down. It doesn't matter if you use cash or credit. If you buy something, or spend any money, write it down! Also on the same page of each week, if you have money coming in, write it down on the bottom of the page, and circle it.

If you break this down weekly, it makes it much easier, and then you can add the totals from each of the 4 weeks.

Now that you have one month of your spending documented, start a new page in your notebook. At the top of the page, write down MONEY SPENT. On the next line down, write down INCOME. Take your paychecks, and any other money that has come in throughout the month.

On the third line subtract your spending from your income. Does the difference surprise you? I can tell you when I did it, it surprised me. I thought I had a good idea of what I spent, but I really had no idea.

So now that you know how much you are bringing in, and how much you are spending, the goal for the next month is to get the spending lower. Think about cutting out fancy dinners, or excessive shopping. Try to pack your lunch for work. Do this for another 30 days, and see if you have made an improvement. If you have, great! If not, keep working at it to get your spending to be less and less every single week.

After you have a handle on what you are spending, now it is time to begin eliminating your debt. A good way to go about this is to eliminate one debt at a time. If you have never heard of the debt snowball, look it up online. It really works, and this is how we have gotten rid of the amount of debt we have. But it works like this; instead of paying a little extra on all of your credit accounts, you are going to take the one that has the lowest balance, and you are going to pay it off. It may take a couple of months, but you are going to focus on paying off the lowest debt first. So make a list of all of your debts. This is an example:

- o Capital One Card Balance: $275.00

- Visa Card: $432.00

- Department Store Credit Card: $245.00

- Department Store Credit Card: $97.00

- Paypal Credit Card: $975.00

- Car loan balance: $7,425.00

- Car loan balance: $5412.00

- Student loan balance: $18,156.00

- Mortgage balance: $179,000.00

- Home Equity loan balance: $9,850.00

We aren't going to look at the total amount of debt, because that is going to overwhelm you, and could cause you to stick your head in the sand again, and we don't want to do that. Instead of ignoring the debt, we are going to take care of it. But, we are going to do it in baby steps, one debt at a time.

So you are going to pick out the debt with the lowest amount due. From the debts I have listed above. The lowest debt is the department store credit card for $97.00. So, when the next payment comes due, we are going to pay extra on that debt. If the minimum due is $20.00, we are going to pay $40.00. We are going to do that until that debt is eliminated. And once it is done, cross that one off of your list.

Then, we are going to find the next debt with the lowest balance. From our example, the next lowest debt is another credit card from a department store with a balance of $245.00. So not only are you going to pay whatever you normally would, and you are going to add to it what you were paying on the first credit card you paid off. So, if you were paying $40.00 on that card, you are going to add $40.00

extra to your payment for the new credit card we are paying off. Once that debt is paid in full, you will move to the next one, continuing to add the extra money that you would have been paying on the previous debts. It really is a debt elimination snowball! I cannot tell you what a good feeling it is to pay off each credit card, or debt, and knowing you are working your way through those debts so you will become debt free. The best way I can describe it is that a HUGE weight has been lifted from your shoulders, and as you continue in your quest, you will feel better, and better, and better. Talk about freedom! But don't take my word for it, do it. Prove it to yourself. You will not be sorry you did.

It can be done, and this is the first checklist you should consider working on to start living a more self-sufficient and prepared lifestyle. But like I stated earlier, the only way you will know this to be true is to do it. So, what are you waiting for? Do it!

Food Storage Checklist, One Step at a Time

It can be very overwhelming, if you let it be that way. But it doesn't have to be. The first thing you need to remember is to stop, and take this one step at a time. If you start preparing one week at a time, and then one month, then three months, before you know it you will have amassed a large amount of supplies, and you will give yourself a little more piece of mind while you continue to build your preps, and also your skills. That's right, having the supplies is only part of the deal. You also have to know how to use them. If you just stock up on random things all the time, you aren't prepping, you're hoarding.

So let's keep things simple, and start slowly, and will move

74

up from there.

Week One

This week's checklist is going to help you get started on buying enough food for a family of four for seven days. All of the items are inexpensive, and mostly pantry items. You can change the list or omit things that you would not usually use. These items can be used for short or longer term food storage

You also need to keep in mind eat what you store, and store what you eat. If you don't normally eat spam or canned tomatoes, don't buy them. Instead find something else that your family will eat.

- o 2 Jars spaghetti sauce ($2.88)
- o 4 packages spaghetti noodles ($3.52)
- o 2 cans canned diced tomatoes ($1.25)
- o 5 lbs white rice ($2.98)
- o 2 lbs dried kidney beans ($1.99)
- o 5 lbs sugar ($2.75)
- o 5 lbs flour ($1.25)
- o 1 container of iodized salt ($.62)
- o 1 container of rapid rise yeast ($3.95)
- o 3 lb of ground beef ($7.99)
- o 1 large fryer chicken ($4.89)
- o 6 cans fruit ($2.97)
- o 6 cans vegetables ($4.08)

- 6 cans cream of chicken or mushroom soup ($5.94)

- 1 large box of instant mashed potatoes ($2.75)

- 2 cans of spam ($2.50)

- 2 boxes scalloped potatoes (1.98)

- 1 large jar applesauce ($1.65)

- 4 gallons water ($3.52)

Grand Total = $59.43

The prices for the food I have listed were actual prices when I purchased them at my local store. Your prices may be higher or lower, depending on what area of the world you live in. And if these are not foods you typically eat, but are willing to give them a try, go for it! Or if you are thinking to yourself while reading my list... "I am NOT eating spam!" Well, then find an alternative that you could substitute. And yes, the food listed may not be the healthiest choices, but they certainly aren't the worst. You can always improvise, go for low sodium versions or gluten free if that is what you are needing. But in the scenario where you don't have anything to eat, you will be grateful for anything, healthy or not.

So now you wonder what on earth are you going to do with this food? Well some of it you are going to eat of course! But some of it you are going to start getting your longer term food pantry stocked up. But right now, we are assuming that you have no food storage, and only have about 3 days of food in your house now.

So with the food you just bought you will be able to make scalloped potatoes and spam, roast chicken, chicken parmesan, hamburger gravy and rice, red beans and rice, spaghetti with meat sauce, chicken and rice casserole, and hamburger pouches. Plus you will have a vegetable, a fruit, and enough flour and yeast to make bread for every meal. If you were to cook from this list, you would have 8 meals. If you include this list into your regular shopping, and do it once a week for a month, you will have enough food for a family of four for three to four weeks! Once you add some extras to your list, and make a diligent effort, you will see how fast your food storage will accumulate.

But let's say you have done this 'extra' shopping for three weeks, and your cupboards are starting to get a little crowded, and you are running out of space for your groceries. Now is the time to find an area inside of your home that you can dedicate to food storage.

The above picture represents a closet that we weren't using so we decided to turn it into a food pantry. You can get creative and it doesn't have to cost a lot of money. You can build your own shelves, but we opted to buy a heavy duty shelving unit because it saved in time and headache rather than building it. However, the next closet that I turn into a food pantry, and my longer term food storage, I will be building the shelves. Yes, it does take more time, but the shelves can be customized as I build them.

One way to save on space for your cans is a can rotator. You can buy these from food storage companies, but they can be really expensive. You can also make your own from cardboard, and make nice can holders, or you can find another alternative.

We found these soda dispensers at Walmart for $4.88 each.

Having your cans in a rotator will help to make sure you use the older cans first, and the newer ones last. You need to continually rotate your food storage, and always use the older items first. Make sure you always check your dates, or you can make it easy on yourself and date each can with a sharpie so you can see the date easily. One way to make sure you use what you store is to go through your food items, and whatever is getting close to expiring, that will become dinner. This can keep your dinners interesting, as well as make it fun while you try to figure out what you are going to make with a can of chicken gravy, canned green beans and cranberries.

So now, you have created a dedicated spot for your longer term food storage. So now, every time you go to the grocery store, you will stock your longer term food storage first, and always keep the older items toward the front so you will use them first.

So now that we have an empty pantry, we need to fill it! This is an example shopping list for stocking up your pantry:

Pantry Stock Up Grocery List

- o   10 cans of soup
- o   2 5lb bags of flour
- o   2 5 lb bags of sugar
- o   2 lb kidney beans
- o   2 lb pinto beans
- o   2 bags 15 bean soup
- o   2 5 lb bags of white rice
- o   10 cans of vegetables

- 10 cans of fruit
- 5 cans canned chicken
- 5 cans of roast beef
- 5 cans tuna
- 4 cans spam
- 5 packages mac-n-cheese
- 1 large package biscuit/baking mix (I like Jiffy)
- 2 bottles maple syrup
- 1 large container quick oats
- 10 packages of different style spaghetti
- 10 different cheap spices
- 2 large packages instant mashed potatoes
- 2 jars chicken bouillon granules
- 2 jars beef bouillon granules
- 5 cans chicken stock
- 2 containers iodized salt
- 5 cake mixes
- 10 gallons water
- 5 packages macaroni (like shells, elbow, rotini)
- 2 vegetable oil
- 1 olive oil
- 1 large container 100% raw honey
- 1 container rapid rise yeast

- o 10 lbs ground beef
- o 2 large fryer chickens
- o 1 large package pork chops
- o 10 cans tomatoes
- o 10 cans crushed tomatoes
- o 10 cans diced tomatoes

Approximate Cost: $250.00

Not bad for a trip to the grocery store to stock up your pantry! Again, this is the approximate cost, and this would be how much it cost me in Colorado, yours maybe less or a little more, depending on where you live. My list will be different from your list, and you will probably be asking why am I buying 2 5lb bags of sugar vs. buying 1 10lb bag of sugar? The reason is because that is what works best for me and my family. You need to do whatever works best for you and your family. There is no right or wrong way to prep, remember that.

You can also save money by stocking up when the items are on sale, but for the sake of keeping this simple, I just want to find the best prices I can for the food I will need right now to keep my pantry full of different types of food while I am fine tuning what else I will need. For me, this a great getting started list of groceries to buy, without anything that is too crazy. And what I mean by that is if you are worried about what others think, or getting the looks in the store because you are buying a cart full of sugar, you don't have to worry if you go to the store and purchase these things! No one will give you a second look, because it looks like normal, everyday items. And that is exactly what it is. Normal everyday items that you are stocking your pantry with.

If you used this list to stock your pantry, and really used the items, this would probably last a family of four about 3-4 weeks, depending on how you were to use it. You will also need to add spices, sauces, and other things for flavor, which I will cover next.

Below is a list of condiments, spices, and sauces that I like to have stocked up in my pantry so I don't run out, and will always have a supply of quick things to grab when I find a recipe that call for something I may not have to make from scratch.

Extras for the Pantry

- 10 fajita spice packs
- 10 chili spice packs
- 10 brown gravy packs
- 10 turkey gravy packs
- 2 large bottle ketchup
- 2 large containers mustard
- 4 jars of pickles
- 2 jars of pickle relish
- 2 bags of brown sugar (and I put it in another larger freezer bag to keep it soft)
- 2 bottles molasses
- 2 jars miracle whip
- 2 large bottles of pepper

- 2 boxes baking soda
- 2 small containers baking powder
- 1 large box cornstarch
- 2 large bottles taco seasoning
- 1 large container chili powder
- 1 large container dried minced garlic
- 1 large container dried cilantro
- 2 bottles ground cumin
- 1 large container white gravy
- 1 package Crisco shortening sticks
- 2 bags chocolate chips
- 1 large container vanilla
- 10 jars of pre-made gravy
- 10 cans green chili
- 2 jars pesto
- 10 cans of mushrooms
- 4 cans black olives
- 3 jars pre-made jam
- 1 large jar peanut butter
- 10 boxes jello
- 5 large boxes pudding
- 2 large containers coffee
- 1 large container hot cocoa mix

- 1 large container non-dairy creamer

- 3 bags marshmallows

- 2 boxes instant flavored oatmeal

This list is a little more expensive than the previous ones, but by keeping my "pre-made" items well stocked, I can grab and go, making meal preparation easier for myself, or my husband if he is the one making the main meal of the day. Also, by having a lot of different spices, and components for making my own sauces and gravies, I can actually stretch our food storage even further.

All of the items I have listed above are all shelf stable, meaning they can last a long time stored on the shelves of my pantry. And yes, there are many items I have purchased that are pre-made, and ready to go, but I do this for a reason. Sometimes you need to have easy to grab and easy to prepare meals. Having these additions helps a lot, and can keep stress levels lower by having extra, and knowing that you do have easy meals you can prepare from your longer term food storage.

So far we have covered items you can buy for your pantry and to keep your short term and longer term food storage. But we cannot leave out long term food storage. And by long term, I mean foods that have a shelf life of 10+ years. Food such as this can be done on your own with food grade storage buckets and gamma lids that fit onto these five gallon pails. You can also purchase food from different companies in large cans. These work great for us, and I can even find them in my local Walmart usually for a very good price. For example, yesterday I went to Walmart, and the had #10 size cans (large) of tvp (textured vegetable protein) chicken and beef flavored for $10.32 a can! That is a great price, and even better, it has a shelf life of 25 years. So needless to say, I will be stopping by Walmart later today to buy a couple of these items. They are from Augason Farms, and I like these products. They have good taste, and I can usually purchase them for less at the store. I have bought from their website when they have good deals, but the shipping time takes forever. So if it is an excellent deal, then yes, I will wait. But if it is only to save a few dollars, I may opt to go pick it up locally.

Like I have said before, this list is an idea. It is what I buy, but that doesn't mean you need to purchase the same things.

Long Term Food for the Pantry

10 size cans

- o 3 Orange Delight Drink Mix
- o 4 Dried Whole Eggs
- o 2 Chocolate Morning Moo's Milk Alternative
- o 4 Honey Coated Banana Slices
- o 2 Freeze Dried Sliced Strawberries
- o 4 Dehydrated Potato Slices
- o 1 Dehydrated Chopped Onions
- o 2 Freeze Dried Sweet Corn
- o 4 Long Grain White Rice

- 2 Dehydrated Potato Dices
- 2 Freeze Dried Broccoli Florets & Stems
- 2 100% Real Instant Nonfat Dry Milk
- 2 TVP Meat Substitute Beef (flavored)
- 1 TVP Meat Substitute Bacon Bits (flavored)
- 2 TVP Meat Substitute Chicken (flavored)
- 2 Cheesy Broccoli Soup Mix
- 3 Creamy Potato Soup Mix
- 3 Chicken Noodle Soup Mix
- 3 Southwest Chili Mix
- 2 Creamy Wheat Cereal
- 4 Buttermilk Pancake Mix
- 2 Freeze Dried Beef Stroganoff
- 2 Freeze Dried Chicken Fettuccini Alfredo
- 2 Spaghetti Marinara with Freeze Dried Beef
- 2 Chili Macaroni with Freeze Dried Beef
- 2 Orange Teriyaki with Freeze Dried Chicken
- 2 Asian Style Teriyaki with Freeze Dried Beef

5 Gallon Pails

- 20 5 gallon food safe buckets
- 20 gamma lids for the buckets
- 20 oxygen absorbers for the buckets
- 20 5 gallon Mylar bags to package the food in

- o   5 Flour

- o   2 Granulated Sugar

- o   2 Spaghetti Pasta

- o   2 Miscellaneous Pasta (1 shells, 1 elbow macaroni)

- o   4 White Rice

- o   1 Kidney Beans

- o   1 Pinto Beans

- o   2 Mixed Beans (made from mixing lots of different types of beans)

And that is my long term food storage. This food storage is designed to last a very long time, which is why I have a lot of #10 cans, along with a lot of 5 gallon pails. So in addition to the food, you will need the supplies to keep it. By packaging your food in the five gallon buckets that have been 'pre-packaged' in Mylar bags, you will be making sure your long term food is safe, and will keep for a very, very long time.

This is the part of being prepared where the cost can really add up, however if you do it one item at a time, you will not need all of the money at one time. So start small, keep breathing and remember, this will not happen overnight, but with perseverance it will happen.

So now we have the basics for beginning food storage, but there are a lot of other things you will need not only to be more prepared, but to feel that way as well.

So let's begin with toiletries, or as some refer to as sundries. If you look up the term 'sundries online, the definition is basically "items that are tiny, an unimportant on their own." As defined by the free dictionary at http://www.thefreedictionary.com/sundries. However, I strongly disagree with that definition, because without these so called un-important items, you would not be able to feed yourself, keep yourself clean, or wipe your you-know-what after doing your business. So as a matter of everyday life, these items are very important, although often overlooked. In a shtf scenario, these comfort items would be even more valuable because they may no longer be available, or maybe too expensive to purchase. Which could be a good thing if you have a lot of these items, because you could use them to barter with.

When I do my shopping, I like to keep to a smaller list, and then build up on it a little bit at a time. I know I keep saying this is what I come up with that is important to me, and for my family. But it's true, and hopefully you will understand to make your list suited to what is important for you and your family.

Try to remember with these items, the cost can add up fast, so look for bargains where you can find them. The Dollar Store may be a good option, but I have found when I buy off brand products here, they aren't very good, and it actually takes more of the product. So even though it may be cheaper when you purchase it, it really won't be when you have to use twice as much. Then it isn't always a great deal. Again, this is my list, and yours may be similar, or completely different. But it is a good tool for you to begin thinking about, and making your own list.

Getting Started Sundries Checklist of Need to Have:

- 24 Rolls of Toilet Paper ($14.00)
- 2 Tubes of Toothpaste ($5.00)
- 3 Bottles of Liquid Dish soap ($3.87)
- 1 Large Box of Baking Soda ($2.99)
- 3 Sticks of Deodorant ($9.98)
- 3 Large Containers of Liquid Laundry Soap ($ 19.97)
- 4 Bottles of Liquid Soap ($3.98)
- 12 Bars of Ivory Bar Soap ($4.99)
- 4 Large Bottles of Shampoo ($15.96)
- 4 Large Bottles of Conditioner ($15.98)
- 4 Large Bottles of Antiseptic Mouthwash – like Listerine ($15.96)
- 5 Boxes of Kleenex ($4.98)
- 4 Bottle Isopropyl Alcohol ($2.72)
- 2 Gallons White Vinegar ($3.44)
- 2 Gallons Bleach ($1.98)
- 1 Large Bottle Apple Cider Vinegar $6.99 for Braggs)
- 1 Large Bottle Olive Oil – yes, it belongs in this category ☺ ($4.99)
- 2 Large Plastic Totes (You can find these free, or for $2.00 or so, check the dollar store)

Total: $140.82

So this list isn't nearly as extensive as the Food prepping area is, however, these items are very important. With this list of items you will be able to clean yourself, and your house for a pretty long time. You will also be wise to stock up on extra towels, both dish towels, and people size towels. But, these can get really expensive, so in order to save money check out your local thrift store. I can usually buy bags of towels for $5.00 a bag, and there will be around 5 to 6 towels per bag. And there isn't anything wrong with them. In some cases, I cut them up to make several dish sized towels, or scrub rags. Also, I bet a lot of you do this, when my towels are too worn out to be used as towels any longer, they get recycled for scrub rags, garage or barn rags.

However you look at the list above, every single item will be used by your family on an everyday basis. Something else to keep in mind is that if we ever do come into a situation where the store shelves are empty, and you run out of commercial cleaners, or even toilet paper, if you have stocked up, it will be no big deal. And another point to remember is that the items on this list could be used as bartering items if they were no longer available on store shelves. I would like to think that a situation like that could never happen, but it has happened before in many different countries around the world. And for me, the risk is just to great that it could happen one day here, so I would rather be safe than without toilet paper.

Another list that will be of benefit for you is for items that will be useful around your house or homestead and they are nice to have now, not just to save for a rainy day. As mentioned before, this list is personalized to the needs of my family, but it may give you a starting point.

Preparedness Items

- Waterproof matches, flint, petroleum jelly and cotton balls(best fire starter), lighters
- Firewood (enough for winter, which could be 4 or 5 cords of wood, that is A LOT of wood.)
- Newspaper, kindling, and fire starters
- Rakes, shovels, hoes, and brooms
- Different types of saws (hand)
- Battery powered tools
- Hand tools
- Gardening tools
- Garden seeds (heirloom- non-hybrid)
- Water storage containers (55 gallon food grade containers)
- Insulation
- Propane grill
- Small cook stove
- Water filters
- Plastic totes
- Percolating coffee maker
- Sleeping bags
- Extra blankets, comforters, and sheets
- Clothes baskets
- Black out plastic for windows
- Extra gas cans (and gas)

- Propane bottles, both large and small (for gas grill, and cook stove)
- Several pairs of heavy duty leather work gloves
- Fix a flat
- Wheel barrel
- Solar lights
- Bandanas
- Fans
- Crank Radio
- Solar generator
- Gas generator
- Heavy rope
- Twine
- Tow rope
- Jumper cables
- Emergency information binder
- Steel wool pads
- Toothbrushes
- Emery boards
- First aid kit
- Feminine hygiene products
- 60 days of prescription medications
- Bug out bags for each person in your family

- Food for your animals, both indoor animals and outside animals
- Pencils, pens, writing paper
- Zip ties
- Paracord
- Multiple knives (Fixed blade knife, folding knife, multi-tool knife)
- Guns with ammunition
- Field storage containers
- Non-lethal defense for your home
- All sizes of batteries (AA, AAA, C, D, 9 volt, hearing aid size, etc)
- Snares
- Night vision
- Duct tape
- Compass
- Solar oven
- Dutch oven
- Paper plates, and disposable silverware
- Extra socks, hats, and gloves
- Sunscreen
- Vitamins (multi, C, D, B12 etc.)
- Fishing gear
- Camping gear

- Candles
- Comfort Items (books, games, magazines, etc.)
- Fly swatters
- Caulk
- Spray paint
- Velcro
- Gorilla Glue (super glue)
- 5 gallon buckets
- Solar battery chargers
- Bug spray
- Portable toilet (composting toilet would be really cool)
- Trash bags
- Bag Balm
- Fire extinguishers
- Tarps
- Clothes pins, and clothes line
- Scissors
- Hand operated can opener (don't get cheap with this, and you should have several)
- Hoses
- Maps
- Cash (emergency fund that you hopefully have in your home)

This list could go on and on, and potentially be as long as this book. No two people will have the same list, but seeing a list like this created might make you think of a few things you will add to your own list.

52 Prepping Projects

So for the mother of all checklists, I thought it would be fun to make a checklist of 52 things you can do on your way to becoming more prepared. You can find instructions all over the internet on how to do each of the projects, and some will take over a week, as we have discussed throughout this section of the book. But it is a general list of things you can do, and it may even inspire you to make your own list.

1. Develop a budget and stick to it
2. Eliminated ¼ of your debt
3. Develop a food pantry for longer term food storage
4. Purchase 5 five gallon buckets with lids to begin long term food storage.
5. Develop a personal book with all of your important information, and all of your emergency contacts. Include addresses and phone numbers of all important friends and relatives.
6. Have 3 different ways to cook food safely.
7. Know 5 different ways to start a fire
8. Create an emergency car kit for every vehicle you own.
9. Create bug out bags for each of your family members (including your pets).

10. Create an emergency cash fund in your, gradually increase it to $1000.00.

11. Find 3 different places you can store enough food and water for your family for a week.

12. Start a compost pile.

13. Start a garden, and grow at least 2 different foods

14. Plant 4 fruit trees

15. Mitigate your property for fire safety (trim back brush, make your exterior as fire proof as you can)

16. Store 150 gallons of water

17. Buy a simple water filter for everyone in your family.

18. Make a simple every day first aid kit for your family.

19. Make a more extensive first aid kit for your family

20. Build a chicken coop (if allowed in your area)

21. Learn 3 alternative heat sources for your home.

22. Inspect all doors, windows and openings for drafts. Repair or replace.

23. Inspect all door locks, and replace if necessary. If there is the possibility someone may have a key to your home, replace all locks. Consider in vesting in deadbolts for added safety.

24. Increase your physical activity, get in shape.

25. Have 2 alternatives of transportation.

26. Build a library for your amassing collection of preparedness and self-reliance books.

27. Organize your garage (or storage area)

28. Get rid of the junk! If you have things you don't use, sell them or get rid of them.

29. Take a hunter safety/gun safety class

30. Service your furnace

31. Bake a loaf of bread

32. Make homemade jelly

33. Can some pickles

34. Safeguard your home, and keep your stuff hidden.

35. Find 4 areas in your home where you could hide some of your food storage.

36. Make your own cleaning supplies, and use them.

37. Purchase a small generator, or make one.

38. Create Jar meals for your food storage.

39. Have 2 different food sources for example fruit and vegetables that you grow, or livestock.

40. Determine if in an emergency you would bug out or bug in, and weigh the pros and cons of each reason. Practice your plan.

41. Know at least 4 ways home, or away from your home in the event of an emergency.

42. Practice being invisible, meaning don't make your home or your preps stand out. Do everything you can think of to keep your preps and your family safe in the event of a major life changing event.

43. Have at least 2 sources of water for your family, for example stored water, and know of at least one other

water source that is not from the water that comes from the pipes in your home.

44. Store at least 10 gallons of gasoline (safely). Start with purchasing gas containers, and have a safe place to store them, then once a week, take an empty gas can with you when you fill up your tank. Add gas stabilizer to it, and number each container. (1,2,3,4...etc) Use the lower numbers first and in order, and when you use it, replace it.

45. Store at least 2 propane tanks (the size that fits your regular gas grill) in a safe place.

46. Go camping for your vacation and take only your skills and supplies with you, try to stay away from modern conveniences.

47. Make extra money using one of your skills, or even by having a yard sale, in order to make enough money for 1 large prep purchase you would really want to have, like a generator, solar electrical system, etc.

48. Store at least 6 months of toiletries,(toilet paper, soap, shampoo, etc) and also have two alternatives for sanitation in case the water stops working.

49. Learn how to knit, and make potholders.

50. Know how to acquire food, such as hunting, fishing, tracking, edible plants, etc.

51. Have three different way to defend yourself and your property.

52. Get to know at least 2 different people that share your concerns, and share the same ideals as you in becoming more prepared. (And not just on the internet)

And now for the mother of all lists! If you are like me, you have researched food storage, and scoured the internet only to never find the magic list you have been looking for, how much food do I need for one year. My way of thinking is, "just tell me what I need to buy, and I'll do it." But unfortunately, I have not been able to find that magic list, so I decided to make my own. Like every other list I have presented to you thus far, this is my own list of what I would need to feed my family. Now what I may have not completely described is that my family amasses a total of 8 people, and if you include extended family it goes up to around 30 people. For the sake of trying to keep things simple, I am going to focus on my immediate family only for this list.

And I want to explain how I came up with the list, and how to make something as intimidating as a year of stored food not seem quite such a large undertaking. I love making lists (if you have not figured that out by now, by the end of this series, I promise you will.) so I made a list of dinners for 30 days.

30 Dinner Ideas:

1.   Cajun Chicken and Sausage with Rice

2.   Jar Chili

3.   Layered Chicken Bake

4.   Porcupine Meatballs

5.   Poppy seed Turkey Bake

6.   Chicken Fajitas

7.   12 Bean Soup

8. Roast Beef over Rice

9. Fish Tacos

10. Hamburger Gravy over Biscuits

11. Bacon Lettuce Tomato Sandwiches on Rolls

12. Reuben Loaf

13. Pasta Tuna Salad and muffins

14. Chicken Cesar Wraps

15. Beef Nachos

16. Camp Pizza

17. Tuna Melts with Chips

18. Chicken Alfredo and Crusty Garlic Bread

19. Mushroom and Wild Rice chicken soup with tortillas

20. Ranch Beans

21. Taco's

22. Spaghetti

23. Sloppy Joes

24. Easy Chicken Pot Pie

25. Sweet and Sour Chow Mein with noodles

26. Chicken, Broccoli, and Rice with Cheese

27. Scalloped Potatoes and Ham (Spam) and cinnamon applesauce

28. Black bean salad with Corn, Rice and Salsa

29. Grilled Cheese and Soup

30. Potato Soup with ham and dumplings

These are just a few ideas, but this is what we will base our year's supply calculations off from. Making a month of dinners really isn't that hard once you sit down to do it. I also make as much of the meal from food storage, or fresh food that we grow ourselves in order to stay more self-reliant, and use what we store.

So if you wanted to, you could take the 30 day dinner menu, and shop this list 12 times, and you would have a year's worth of food for your family. This is how I like to do it, it keeps it manageable, and I do not get overwhelmed in thinking how much a year's worth of groceries is going to cost, because let's face it, THAT could be scary, and may cause you to stick your head in the sand again like a lot of others who don't want to be woken up.

SO even though this is a list of shopping for one year's worth of food, you could break it down into a smaller more manageable shopping trip, or buy one item at a time. There is no right or wrong way really12 times what you could need for a year, it is definitely the closest list I have ever found to give you an idea of how much food you will really need.

1 Year of Food Grocery Shopping List:

Meats:

- o Canned Chicken (80 cans)

- Canned Roast Beef (60 cans)
- Canned Ham (40 cans)
- Canned Spam (20 cans)
- Canned Tuna (40 cans)
- Canned Bacon (24 cans)
- TVP Chicken 4 #10 Cans)
- TVP Beef (4 #10 Cans)
- Canned Corn Beef (15 cans)
- Ground Beef (50 lbs)

Staples:

- Flour (500 lbs)
- Sugar (150 lbs)
- Rice (150 lbs)
- Mixed dried beans, pinto, kidney, black, etc. (150 lbs)
- Yeast (10 Jars)
- Powdered milk (50 lbs)
- Spices (at least 2 large containers each)
- Honey (1 gallon)
- Coffee (50 lbs)
- Salt (20 lbs)
- Pepper (4 large containers)
- Baking Soda (10 lbs)
- Baking Powder (5 lbs)

- Cornstarch (10 lbs)
- Baking Mix (8 boxes)
- Spaghetti Noodles (10 boxes)
- Fettuccini Noodles (10 boxes)
- Rolled Oats (50 lbs)
- Pancake Syrup (4 gallons)
- 5 gallon buckets with gamma lids (40)
- Oxygen Absorbers 300cc (100)
- Mylar Bags for 5 gallon buckets (40)

Canned Vegetable and Fruits

- Cut Green Beans (80 cans)
- French Style Green Beans (60 cans)
- Corn (80 cans)
- Creamed Corn (20 cans)
- Potatoes (60 cans)
- Mixed Vegetables (40 cans)
- Carrots (20 cans)
- Beets (10 cans)
- Applesauce (8 large containers)
- Peaches (80 cans)
- Pears (60 cans)
- Fruit Cocktail (60 cans)
- Pineapple (20 cans)

- Spaghetti Sauce (20 cans)
- Stewed tomatoes (25 cans)
- Diced Tomatoes (25 cans)
- Tomato Sauce (25 cans)

This list is not complete, and yes, there are a lot of canned goods, and staples, and yes, parts of these items will last for more than a year. However, some will be depleted, and in that event you may be thinking then what? What happens if all of your canned tomatoes are used up by the end of the year and there are no more tomatoes on the store shelves? Or you lose your job and aren't able to replenish your pantry? While the list of food is a good start, it is never complete. You will always be tweaking, or making changes to your own food storage to what you need it to be.

And when your original food storage starts to dwindle, think about other ways to replace it. You will notice on our list of storage items, we don't have a lot of eggs. This is because we have a flock of chickens, which will provide fresh eggs for our family.

One part of food storage is providing fresh components to your everyday meals. In our climate, our growing season is not year round, so in order to supplement and to make sure we are always building into our food storage, we have a lot of canned items. But then when spring rolls around, and I am able to get out and plant my garden, and then later harvest from my garden, I will replenish items for my pantry by freezing and canning.

Although this list should be changed to suit your needs, it

will give you a good generalized starting point in order to give yourself the security of having food storage, and many options for creating meals for you and your family.

This is by no means an all complete list of everything related to living a more prepared lifestyle, but it gives you a basic idea of some areas that you will be able to use, and incorporate in your everyday life. You may not feel that you are a prepper, and may not classify yourself as such. But be taking responsibility for yourself and your family, not only are you on the road to a more self-reliant lifestyle, but you will also be well on your way to taking control of your life.

Just think about the freedom you will feel in knowing you have enough food to sustain your family for 6 months, or even a year. Think about what it would feel like to have all of your debts paid off, and not have to go work every day because you have too, but because you want to.

Think about it, if you could have a job that you loved, and enjoyed, and you didn't have to rely on your paycheck to make sure you were getting by every month. Do yourself and your family a favor, get off the merry go round, and take control of your own life. Take the responsibility and control back. Don't rely on getting help from the government, or others. Rely on yourself for the things you can do yourself and continue to learn so your self-reliance grows and grows.

CAMPING

Camping is probably one of the best ways to practice your survival and preparedness skills. Not only are you spending time getting back to nature and away from the technical pace of normal everyday life, but you are also able to put to use the skills you have been acquiring while you are becoming more prepared.

Going out for a weekend campout is fun, and many of us can remember fondly outings that we have has with our families. If you don't have any memories of going camping, now is the time to start creating those special times with your family. You don't have to spend a lot of money, and you can usually get out of town for the weekend fairly easily, depending on what part of the world you live in.

If you aren't ready to completely 'rough-it' quite yet, start smaller and find a cabin out in the woods that you can rent for the weekend. It won't be quite the same, but if it's your first outing and you're not sure how ready you are, it might be a great way to break yourself into camping slowly, and while still having some modern conveniences of home.

But if you are ready to go, here is a list of things you will need to have when planning your outing to make the most of it, and have a great time:

- Tent
- Sleeping bags
- Flashlights
- Cook stove
- Folding chairs and table
- Cooking utensils (pots, fry pan, coffee pot, etc)
- Eating utensils (plates, silverware, cups, etc.)
- Fire starting equipment

- Camping lanterns
- Pillows
- Trash bags
- Bottled water
- Easy cook food
- Fishing gear
- Hiking gear
- Hunting gear
- First aid kit
- Cold weather clothing
- Rain gear
- Towels, rags, etc.
- Snacks
- Playing cards, board games (I like to call them "bored" games)

This list is not all inclusive, but it gives you a general idea of what you will need in order to camp for a weekend with your family. You can modify, or add or delete items as you need, and make it what you need for a fun filled family weekend with your family, or even a quite getaway for you and your significant other.

If you aren't into fishing, then focusing on hiking, or vice versa. But the main objective is for you to practice the skills you have already acquired, and possibly add a few more to your list. If you have never created a fire, this is the perfect opportunity for you to practice. But don't practice one way to make fire, try at least 3 or 4 different ways to make a fire.

If you have never cooked over a campfire, again try at least three different ways of cooking out in the open. With practice and a lot of outings you will not only become proficient in camping, but also in useable skills that will be valuable in an emergency or disaster type situation.

Accumulating camping equipment can be done very affordably. You could choose to buy camping items new from big chain stores, or you can be a little more frugal and scope out yard sales or thrift stores. By opting for the less expensive option, you are going to get a lot more equipment for your money. Plus, if it's already used, you aren't going to be too worried about it getting dirty or used during your campout. And once you have started collecting your camping gear, grab some plastic totes to store your items in put them into your garage or storage area, and they will be ready to go whenever you feel the urge to go camping.

Getting away with your family can strengthen family bonds, and bring the focus back to what really is important, your family. No matter what is going on in the world, and the latest gadgets, and what your neighbors have, nothing will replace your family. So weekend getaways can help to strengthen the bond of what a family really is. It will also give you a new, or renewed perspective on why you are doing what you are doing, it's for your family. When things seem overwhelming, or you feel sad, remember your family is there for you, and plan a camping trip!

You will not only build confidence in your preparedness skills, but you will gain a new perspective on the beauty of the world around you.

CAR KITS

Unless you are living in an Amish community, there is a pretty good chance that you have a vehicle which you will be relying on to get you to your job, and transport your family. No matter where you live, if you have a vehicle, you need to have an emergency kit in your vehicle. Don't wait until you need it before you make it. Do it now. It is a simple kit to complete, and you can stick it in your trunk, and feel a little bit better knowing you have at least some supplies in your trunk in case of an emergency. Think of it as if you are preparing a bug out bag for your car.

To get started, you will need a crate, or something to store everything in. I have no idea of where I found these, but I have had them forever, and they work great for storing stuff in your trunk. They have handles, and are small enough to fit in most trunks, and they allow for a lot of storage.

As you can see, I have two in my car. One is for items my car may need, and the other keeps extra supplies for me, just in case. By keeping the two crates separate, I can keep toxic items away from my personal use items like food, medical kit, and things that I can use for myself in my car.

This is how I have my crates broken down:

Car Care Crate

- Oil
- Windshield wiper fluid
- Ready to use antifreeze
- 1 can of fix a flat
- Oil rags
- Small tool kit
- Funnel
- Brake fluid
- 1 gallon of water
- Jumper Cables
- Towing strap
- Foldable shovel

Personal Care Crate

- Medical (First Aid Kit)
- Get home bag with supplies
- Blanket
- Boots
- Waterproof matches

- o Canned food
- o Can opener
- o Gloves
- o Hat
- o Coat
- o Umbrella
- o Drinks
- o Twine from hay bales
- o Prescription medications (that can be in the heat or cold)
- o Pens, paper and pencils

It seems pretty basic, and it is. But that's the point. Take a few minutes, gather these items and put them in your car. You have most of these items in your home, and if you get stranded or stuck, these things will not help you when they are on your garage shelf.

Depending on where you live will help determine what kind of items you keep in your emergency trunk kit. But I feel it is safe to say some items like the fluids for your car, fix a flat, and a small tool kit are very smart additions to keep in your vehicle at all times. Not only do you need to put the items in your trunk, you should check on them periodically. If you end up using any of the items, make sure to replace what you have used.

In addition to the two crates I keep in my trunk, there are a couple of other things that I like to have. Kitty litter, and empty gas can, and a tarp. The tarp has a lot of different uses, from providing shade if you are on a barren stretch of road and it is 110 degrees outside, to providing shelter, and you can even use it as a makeshift sled, or carry heavy objects, if you needed too. The kitty litter is helpful in the winter if you ever get stuck. Sometimes putting some kitty litter under a shoveled out tire can give you enough traction to get unstuck. And the empty gas can will be needed in the event you run out of gas. I know, it seems pretty straightforward, but you never know. And after all, that is what we are all about, is being more prepared, right?

ABOUT THE AUTHOR

My path to prepping started when I was little. My parents made it a part of my life, so I grew up thinking it was "normal" to do things like make your own clothes, or cook in a wood stove, and milk cows. But sadly, as I grew up I fell out of that way of thinking, and that way of life.

But after I started my own family, and moved to a rural community, I quickly realized that being prepared for whatever country living could throw at you was much easier than relying on someone else. Even though I had not been living this lifestyle for about 20 years, the things I did learn came back to me. I found myself researching how to make my own butter and bread, and how to can. I learned the good and not so good ways to butcher a chicken and work my garden.

And the more I started doing for myself, I really understood what it meant to be happy. There is a lot to be said for a hard day's work, and taking pride in what you have done. I work hard at trying to find ways to be more self-reliant, and I am grateful that my husband feels the same way. Together we find new ways to save money, store food, learn about security and just live a better life with less.

You don't have to make millions of dollars to be happy, but you do have to be happy with what you have. I have learned so much from others, and through my own trial and errors. Now that doesn't mean it's all easy, and everything works the first time. But it has taught me to never give up and keep on trying, because success may only be one tiny mistake away.

Knowing what I know now, when I first got started, I wished I would have had the vast amount of resources that are available now. With the ever changing environment of the world, and even the country we live in today, I feel it is so important to reach as many people as possible, and share what I have learned because maybe it will help someone else, and make a difference in their life.

So I challenge you, as I have challenged myself. Make it a priority to become more prepared and self-reliant. This isn't something that you will be able to complete overnight, in a week, or even a month. Being prepared and self-reliant is a lifestyle that is best looked at as a marathon, and not a sprint. The more time you take and invest into it, the more you will get out of it. And the best part of all of this is you will really be setting yourself free, because you will have accepted responsibility for your future. You will not be relying on someone else, and the more prepared you are, the less you will worry. The less you worry, the happier you will be.

Here's to your happiness and path to preparedness!

-Lisa Goodwin

Upcoming Work

This book is the third in a series of how to be more prepared and live a more self-reliant lifestyle. Be on the lookout for future books for every letter of the alphabet. Here is a short list of upcoming titles:

D- Diet, Dogs, Darkness, Death and Dying, Disasters, Disabilities, Diapers and Defense

E- Education, Eggs, Edible Landscaping, Ears and Eating the Elephant

F- Food Storage, Fencing, Food Forest, Fun, First-Aid, Fire Mitigation, Friends and Family

G- Guns, Garbage, Garages, Gardening, Get Home Bag, Gold, Goats, and Government

H- Home Security, Homemade Cleaners, Herbs, Haircuts, Horses, and Honeybees

I- Ice, Income, Insulation, Infections, Intruders, Investing, and Innovation

And much, much more to come! 26 letters of the alphabet means 26 books on being prepared and more self-reliant. If you would like to be undated of when the future books become available, send us an email and we will put you on our email list of upcoming releases.

Resources

All of the resources listed below are from places I have purchased. I have not solicited any advertising from the companies, and I do not get anything out of listing them here. I have put them down here because I have used them myself, and they have great service. Please use these as a guideline, but if you can find what you are looking for somewhere else, and you like the company, that is where I would go to purchase the items.

Augason Farms: http://www.augasonfarms.com/

Grover Rocket Stove: http://www.amazon.com/Heavy-Duty-Grover-Rocket-Stove/dp/B007FZKTQ8/ref=sr_1_1?ie=UTF8&qid=1387039544&sr=8-1&keywords=rocketstove

Volcano Grill: http://beprepared.com/volcano-ii-collapsible-stove.html?sc=GOOGLE&oc=GOOG008015&gclid=CMXVncOTsLsCFcxAMgodPWkAJQ

Wilson's Worms (Red Wigglers): http://www.wilsonsworms.com/

Grown Locally (Black Soldier fly larva): http://www.grownlocally.net/shop/

Ball Blue Book Guide to Preserving: http://www.walmart.com/ip/17203433?wmlspartner=wlpa&selectedSellerId=3&adid=22222222227010783515&wl0=&

wl1=g&wl2=c&wl3=40638562750&wl4=&wl5=pla&wl6=38
843501950&veh=sem

□

www.ingramcontent.com/pod-product-compliance
Lightning Source LLC
Chambersburg PA
CBHW070155290526
45789CB00002B/774